This journal belongs to:

How to use this journal

The Present Planner is designed to help you stay on top of present-giving, ensuring that every gift you give is thoughtful, meaningful and perfectly timed.

The 'Year Calendar' provides space to note down important dates, such as birthdays, anniversaries and other notable gifting occasions. A clear view of the year ahead will make sure you never miss a special event.

You'll find space to collect your gifting inspiration in the 'Gifting Ideas' section with a place to record ideas and their potential recipients. The 'Great Places' section will help you remember any shops or websites you have visited that are especially good for buying gifts.

Create dedicated logs for the people you give to in the 'Gifts By Recipient' section. Complete with details such as birthdays or anniversaries, their likes and any gifting ideas. With space to record past gifts given, you can avoid duplication and ensure that each gift is unique and thoughtful.

There is even a space to jot down any present ideas you may have for yourself in the 'My Wishlist' section.

Index

Year Calendar 5

Gifting Ideas 11

Great Places 15

Gifting Index 19

Gifts By Recipient 23

My Wishlist 115

Year Calendar

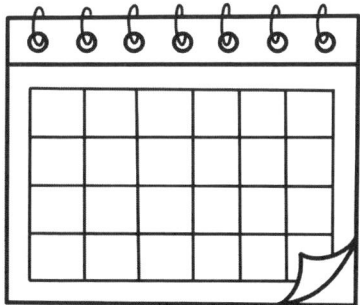

January

February

March

April

May

June

July

August

September

October

November

December

Gifting Ideas

Ideas...

Ideas I Have Seen	Who Might Like Them?

Ideas I Have Seen	Who Might Like Them?

Great Places

Shops Worth a Visit...

Shop name	Location

Websites of Note . . .

Website

Gifting Index

Gift List By Person...

Page	Name	Birthday

Page	Name	Birthday

Gifts By Recipient

Recipient...

Name: ....

Date(s): ....

Likes

Ideas/Wishlist

Date	Gift

Recipient...

Name: ....

Date(s): ....

Likes

Ideas/Wishlist

Date	Gift

Recipient...

Name: ....

Date(s): ....

Likes

Ideas/Wishlist

Date	Gift

Recipient...

Name: ....

Date(s): ....

Likes

Ideas/Wishlist

Date	Gift

Recipient...

Name: ....

Date(s): ....

Likes

Ideas/Wishlist

Date	Gift

Recipient...

Name: ....

Date(s): ....

Likes

....
....
....
....
....
....
....
....

Ideas/Wishlist

....
....
....
....
....
....
....
....
....
....
....
....
....
....

Date	Gift

Recipient...

Name: ....

Date(s): ....

Likes

Ideas/Wishlist

Date	Gift

Recipient...

Name: ....

Date(s): ....

Likes

Ideas/Wishlist

Date	Gift

Recipient...

Name: ....

Date(s): ....

Likes

Ideas/Wishlist

Date	Gift

Recipient...

Name: ....

Date(s): ....

Likes

Ideas/Wishlist

Date	Gift

Recipient...

Name: ....

Date(s): ....

Likes

Ideas/Wishlist

Date	Gift

Recipient...

Name: ....

Date(s): ....

Likes

Ideas/Wishlist

Date	Gift

Recipient...

Name: ....

Date(s): ....

Likes

Ideas/Wishlist

Date	Gift

Recipient...

Name: ....

Date(s): ....

Likes

Ideas/Wishlist

Date	Gift

Recipient...

Name: ....

Date(s): ....

Likes

Ideas/Wishlist

Date	Gift

Recipient...

Name: ....

Date(s): ....

Likes

Ideas/Wishlist

Date	Gift

Recipient...

Name: ....

Date(s): ....

Likes

....
....
....
....
....
....
....
....

Ideas/Wishlist

....
....
....
....
....
....
....
....
....
....
....
....
....
....

Date	Gift

Recipient...

Name: ....

Date(s): ....

Likes

Ideas/Wishlist

Date	Gift

Recipient...

Name: ....

Date(s): ....

Likes

Ideas/Wishlist

Date	Gift

Recipient...

Name: ....

Date(s): ....

Likes

Ideas/Wishlist

Date	Gift

Recipient...

Name: ....

Date(s): ....

Likes

Ideas/Wishlist

Date	Gift

Recipient...

Name: ....

Date(s): ....

Likes

....
....
....
....
....
....
....
....

Ideas/Wishlist

....
....
....
....
....
....
....
....
....
....
....
....
....
....
....

Date	Gift

Recipient...

Name: ....

Date(s): ....

Likes

Ideas/Wishlist

Date	Gift

Recipient...

Name: ....

Date(s): ....

Likes

....
....
....
....
....
....
....
....

Ideas/Wishlist

....
....
....
....
....
....
....
....
....
....
....
....
....
....

Date	Gift

… Recipient…

Name:

Date(s):

Likes

Ideas/Wishlist

Date	Gift

Recipient...

Name: ....

Date(s): ....

Likes

Ideas/Wishlist

Date	Gift

Recipient...

Name: ....

Date(s): ....

Likes

Ideas/Wishlist

Date	Gift

Recipient...

Name: ....

Date(s): ....

Likes

Ideas/Wishlist

Date	Gift

Recipient...

Name: ....

Date(s): ....

Likes

Ideas/Wishlist

Date	Gift

Recipient...

Name: ....

Date(s): ....

Likes

Ideas/Wishlist

Date	Gift

Recipient...

Name: ....

Date(s): ....

Likes

Ideas/Wishlist

Date	Gift

Recipient...

Name: ....

Date(s): ....

Likes

Ideas/Wishlist

Date	Gift

Recipient...

Name: ....

Date(s): ....

Likes

Ideas/Wishlist

Date	Gift

Recipient...

Name: ....

Date(s): ....

Likes

Ideas/Wishlist

Date	Gift

Recipient...

Name: ....

Date(s): ....

Likes

Ideas/Wishlist

Date	Gift

Recipient...

Name: ....

Date(s): ....

Likes

....
....
....
....
....
....
....
....

....
....
....
....
....
....
....
....

Ideas/Wishlist

....
....
....
....
....
....
....
....
....
....
....
....
....
....
....
....

Date	Gift

Recipient...

Name: ....

Date(s): ....

Likes

Ideas/Wishlist

Date	Gift

Recipient...

Name: ....

Date(s): ....

Likes

Ideas/Wishlist

Date	Gift

Recipient...

Name: ....

Date(s): ....

Likes

Ideas/Wishlist

Date	Gift

Recipient...

Name: ....

Date(s): ....

Likes

Ideas/Wishlist

Date	Gift

Recipient...

Name: ....

Date(s): ....

Likes

Ideas/Wishlist

Date	Gift

Recipient...

Name: ....

Date(s): ....

Likes

Ideas/Wishlist

Date	Gift

Recipient...

Name: ....

Date(s): ....

Likes

Ideas/Wishlist

Date	Gift

Recipient...

Name: ....

Date(s): ....

Likes

Ideas/Wishlist

Date	Gift

Recipient...

Name: ....

Date(s): ....

Likes

Ideas/Wishlist

Date	Gift

My Wishlist

My Wishlist . . .

THE PRESENT PLANNER

Let's Get Organised collection, first published by FROM YOU TO ME LTD in September 2024

For a full range of all our titles where gifts can also be personalised, please visit

WWW.FROMYOUTOME.COM

FROM YOU TO ME are committed to a sustainable future for our business, our customers and our planet. This book is printed and bound in Malaysia on FSC® certified paper.

All rights reserved. No part of this publication may be reproduced, stored in a retrieval system, or transmitted in any form or by any means electronic, mechanical, photocopying, recording, or otherwise, without the prior written permission of the copyright owner who can be contacted via the publisher at the above website address.

3 5 7 9 11 13 15 14 12 10 8 6 4 2

Copyright © 2024 FROM YOU TO ME LTD

ISBN 978-1-907048-79-1

FROM YOU TO ME LTD, STUDIO 100, THE OLD LEATHER FACTORY
GLOVE FACTORY STUDIOS, HOLT, WILTSHIRE, BA14 6RJ